Vocal • Piano

NANCY LAMOTT

ORIGINAL KEYS for SINGERS

Many thanks to Christopher Marlowe for providing the arrangements used in this book.
For transpositions or for transcriptions of other arrangements by Christopher Marlowe,
email Christopher Marlowe at
chris@chrismarlowe.com.

Photo of Nancy LaMott by Stephen Mosher

ISBN 978-1-4234-5688-9

HAL•LEONARD®
CORPORATION
7777 W. BLUEMOUND RD. P.O. BOX 13819 MILWAUKEE, WI 53213

Visit Hal Leonard Online at
www.halleonard.com

When Nancy LaMott died, at the age of 43, in 1995, she left behind 5 magnificent CD's filled with classic songs, beautifully arranged and played by her music director, Christopher Marlowe. She also left behind numerous other recordings of her signature songs, which through the years have been, and will continue to be, released as posthumous CD's.

Over the years, I, as her producer, have received many requests for those arrangements from singers and fans all over the world. Now at last, thanks to Hal Leonard, many of Nancy's most famous arrangements are available in one book, exactly as Christopher Marlowe played them.

DAVID FRIEDMAN

For more information on Nancy LaMott's CD's, her story, and on projects related to her legacy, please go to NancyLamott.com.

AUTUMN LEAVES/ WHEN OCTOBER GOES

AUTUMN LEAVES
English lyric by JOHNNY MERCER
French lyric by JACQUES PREVERT
Music by JOSEPH KOSMA

WHEN OCTOBER GOES
Words by JOHNNY MERCER
Music by BARRY MANILOW

old win - ter's song. _____ But I miss you most of all, my dar - ling, _____ when au - tumn leaves start to fall. _____ And when Oc - to - ber goes

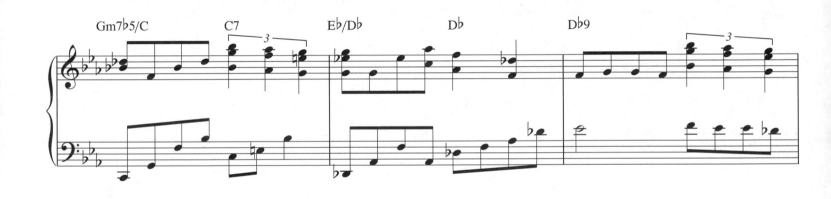

And when Oc - to - ber goes ___

DOWNTOWN

Words and Music by
TONY HATCH

HELP IS ON THE WAY

Words and Music by
DAVID FRIEDMAN

Smoothly but with movement

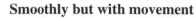

Don't give up ___ the ship _____ e - ven when you feel ___ it's

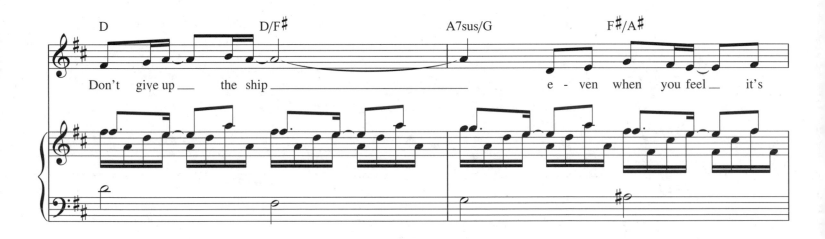

sink - ing _____ and you don't ___ know what to do. ___

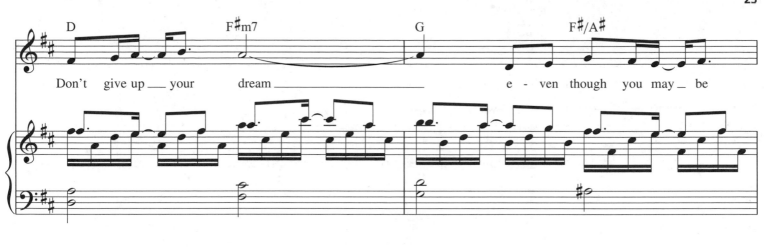

Don't give up ___ your dream _____ e - ven though you may _ be

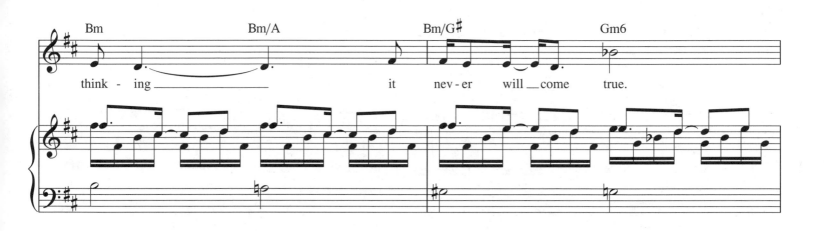

think - ing _____ it nev - er will ___ come true.

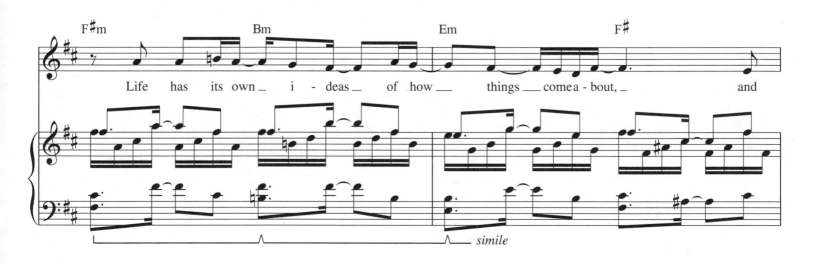

Life has its own ___ i - deas ___ of how ___ things ___ come a - bout, ___ and

simile

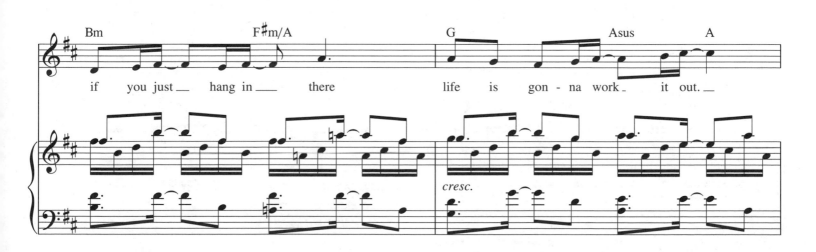

if you just ___ hang in ___ there life is gon - na work ___ it out. ___

cresc.

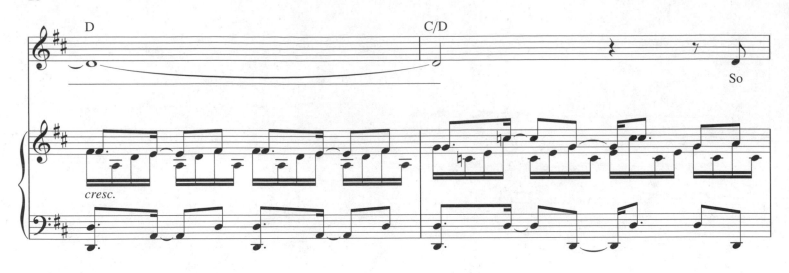

So

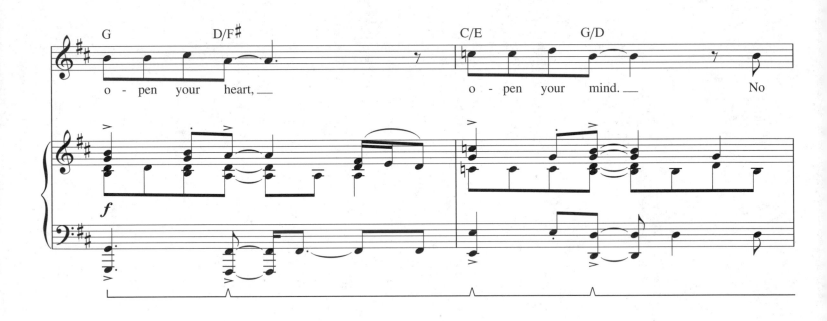

o - pen your heart, ___   o - pen your mind. ___   No

mat - ter how _ you've tried and failed, _   to - mor - row you _ could turn _ and find _ that

I GOT THE SUN IN THE MORNING

from the Stage Production ANNIE GET YOUR GUN

Words and Music by
IRVING BERLIN

And with the sun in the morn-ing and the moon in the eve-ning

I'm all right.

Got no diam - ond, got no pearl, still I think__ I'm a

luck-y girl.__ I got the sun_____ in the morn-ing and the

I ____

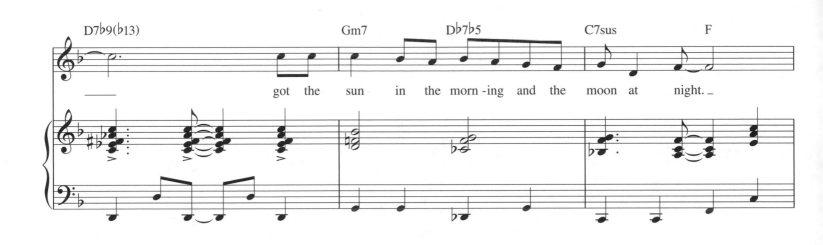

____ got the sun in the morn-ing and the moon at night. __

And with the sun in the

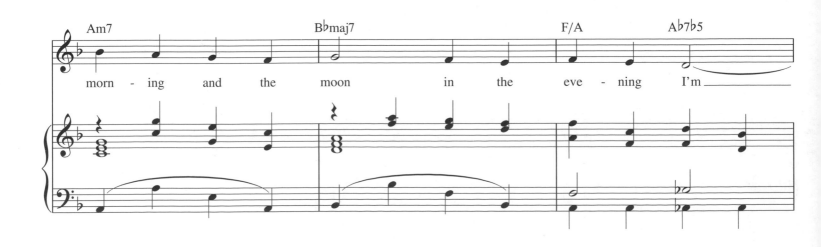

morn-ing and the moon in the eve-ning I'm ____

I HAVE DREAMED

from THE KING AND I

Lyrics by OSCAR HAMMERSTEIN II
Music by RICHARD RODGERS

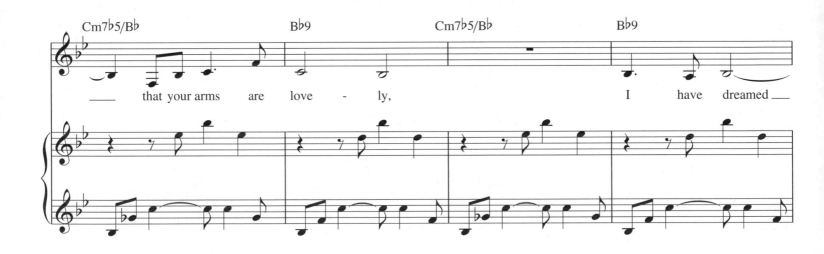

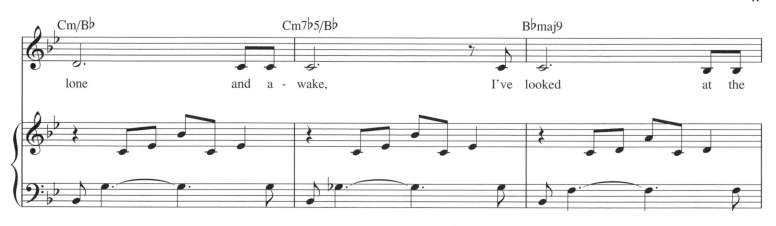

lone and a - wake, I've looked at the

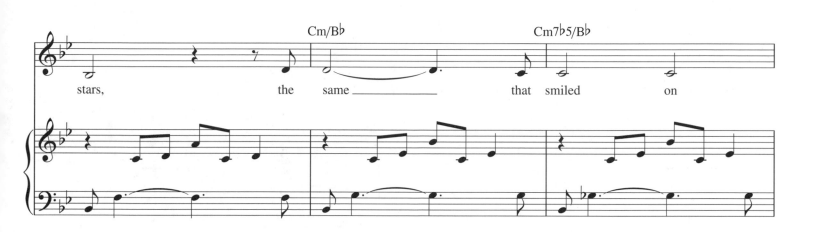

stars, the same ___ that smiled on

you. ___ And time and a -

gain, I've thought all the things that

I'LL BE HERE WITH YOU

Words and Music by
DAVID FRIEDMAN

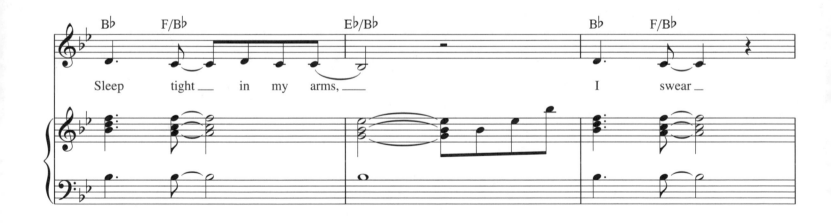

don't be a-fraid,___ sleep safe in my arms.___

Ba - by,___ you'll be O K,___ I'll keep__ you from harm.___

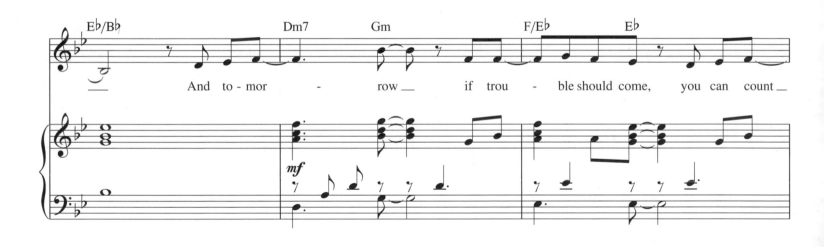

And to-mor - row__ if trou - ble should come, you can count__

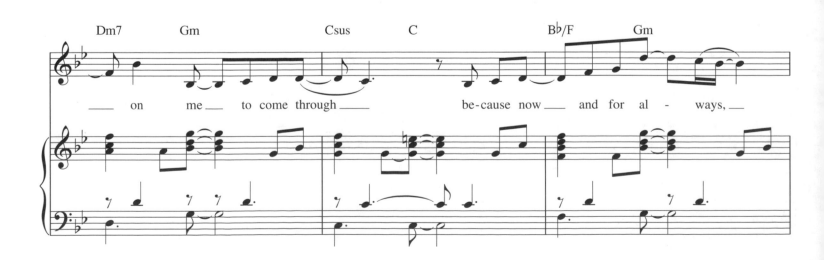

___ on me to come through ___ be-cause now__ and for al - ways,___

IT MIGHT AS WELL BE SPRING

from STATE FAIR

Lyrics by OSCAR HAMMERSTEIN II
Music by RICHARD RODGERS

I'm as rest-less as a wil-low in a wind-storm,
I am star-ry-eyed and vague-ly dis-con-tent-ed,

I'm as jump-y as a pup-pet on a string.
like a night-in-gale with-out a song to sing.

I'd swear that I had spring fe-ver, _____ but I
Oh, why do I have spring fe-ver _____ when it

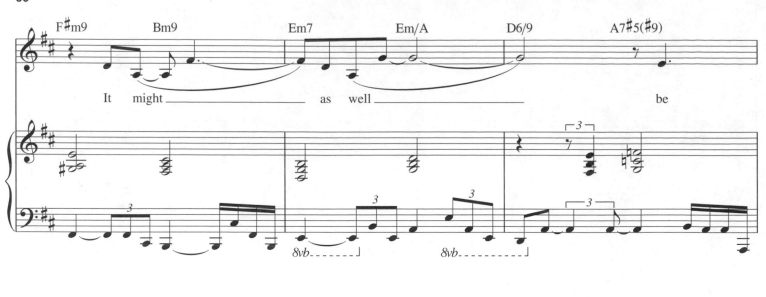

It might _____ as well _____ be

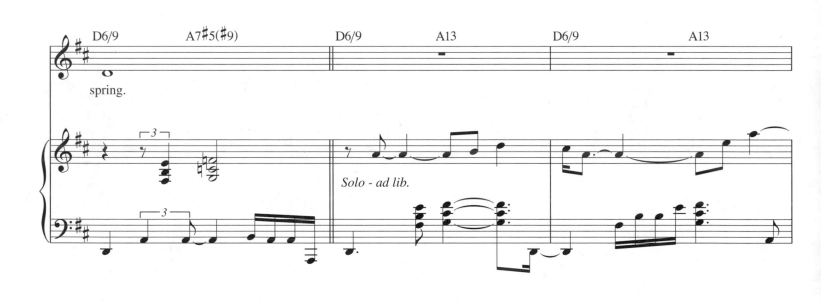

spring.

Solo - ad lib.

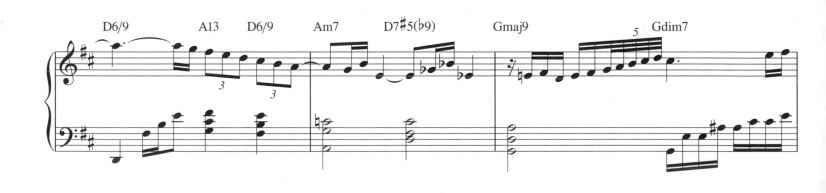

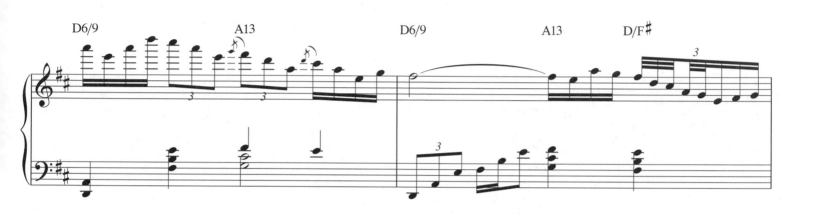

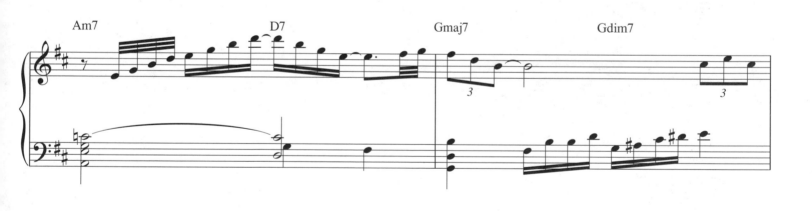

I _____ keep wish-ing _____ I were some - where _____ else,

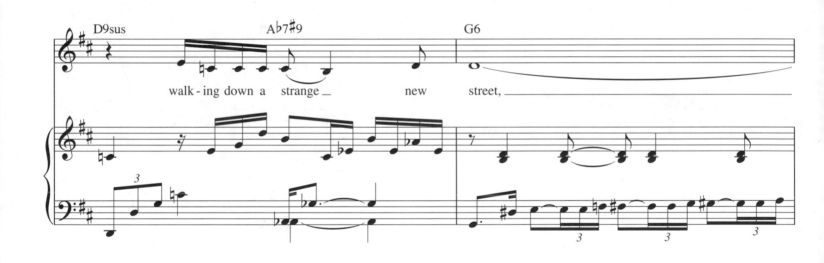

walk-ing down a strange _____ new street, _____

_____ hear-ing words _____ that I have nev-er heard _____

MOON RIVER

from the Paramount Picture BREAKFAST AT TIFFANY'S

Words by JOHNNY MERCER
Music by HENRY MANCINI

JUST IN TIME FOR CHRISTMAS

Music by DAVID FRIEDMAN
Lyrics by DAVID ZIPPEL

LISTEN TO MY HEART

Words and Music by
DAVID FRIEDMAN

NO MOON AT ALL/OLD DEVIL MOON

NO MOON AT ALL
By DAVE MANN
and REDD EVANS

No moon at all, ___ what a night, e - ven light-'ning bugs have dimmed their lights. _

OLD DEVIL MOON
from FINIAN'S RAINBOW
Words by E.Y. "Yip" HARBURG
Music by BURTON LANE

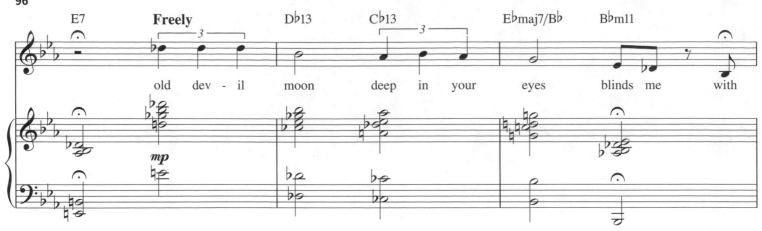

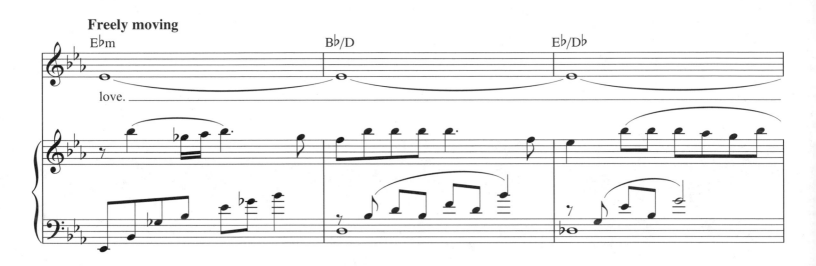

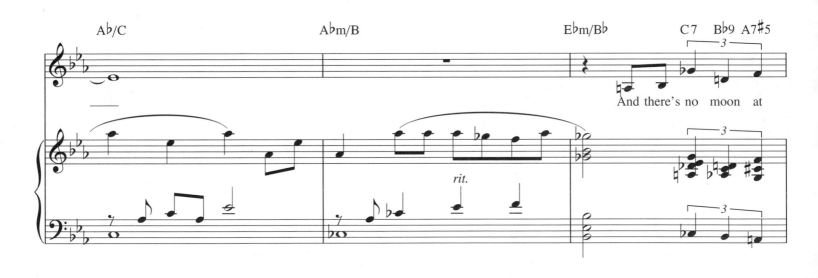

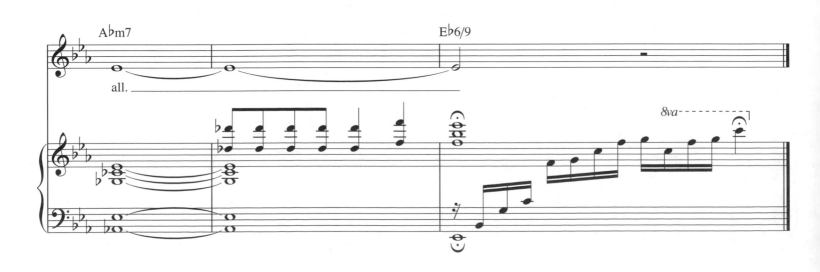

THAT OLD BLACK MAGIC

from the Paramount Picture STAR SPANGLED RHYTHM

Words by JOHNNY MERCER
Music by HAROLD ARLEN

Slowly

That

old black mag - ic has me in its spell, that old black mag - ic that you weave so well. Those

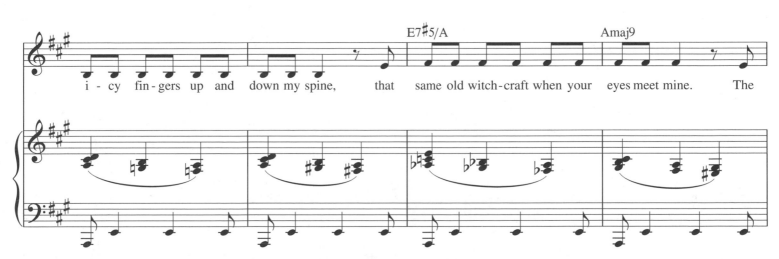

i - cy fin - gers up and down my spine, that same old witch - craft when your eyes meet mine. The

same old tin-gle that I feel in-side, and then that el-e-va-tor starts its ride. And

down and down I go, round and round I go, like a leaf that's caught in the tide.

I should stay a-way, but what can I do? I hear your

name and I'm a-flame, a-flame with such a burn-ing de-

OUT OF THIS WORLD/SO IN LOVE

from the Motion Picture OUT OF THIS WORLD

Out of This World
Lyric by JOHNNY MERCER
Music by HAROLD ARLEN

SO IN LOVE
from KISS ME, KATE
Words and Music by
COLE PORTER

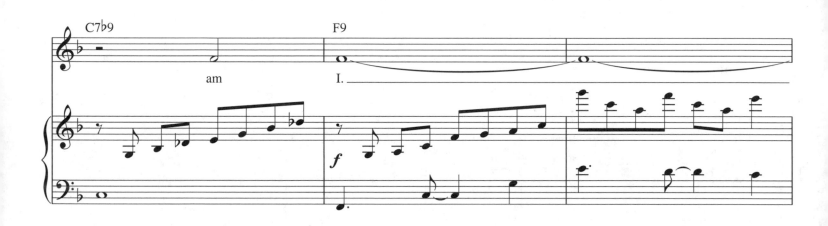

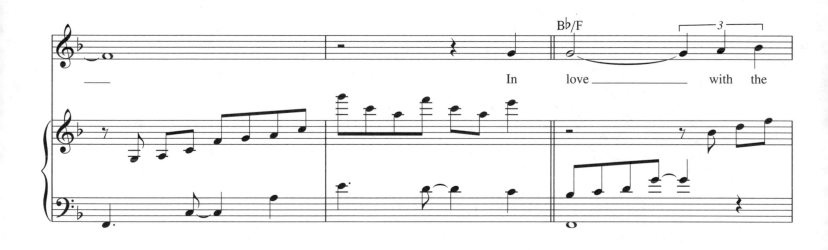

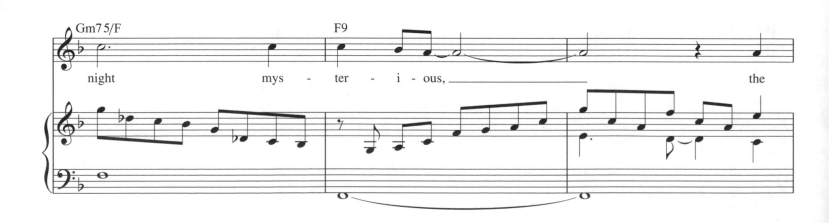

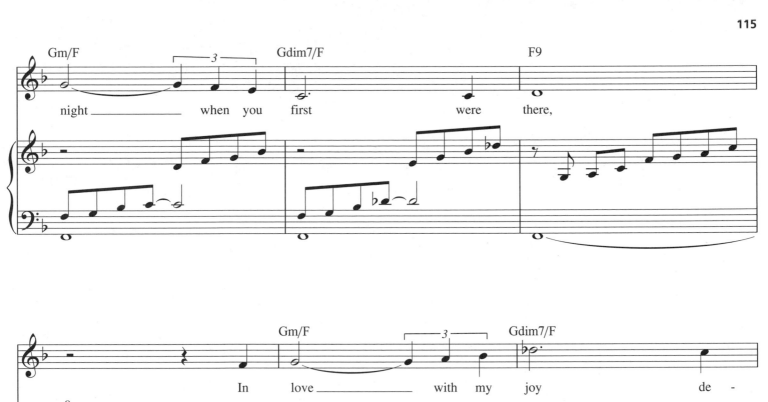

night _____ when you first _____ were there,

In love _____ with my joy de -

lir - i - ous _____ when I knew that

you could care. _____

SKYLARK

Words by JOHNNY MERCER
Music by HOAGY CARMICHAEL

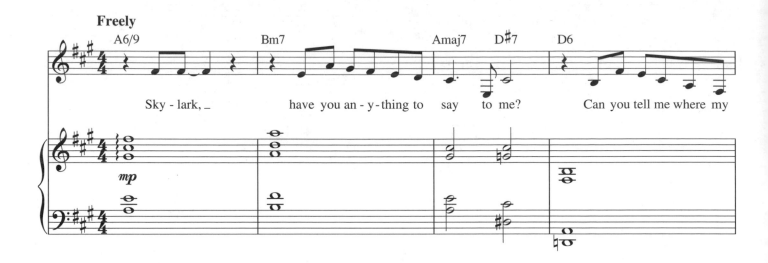

Sky - lark, _ have you an - y-thing to say to me? Can you tell me where my

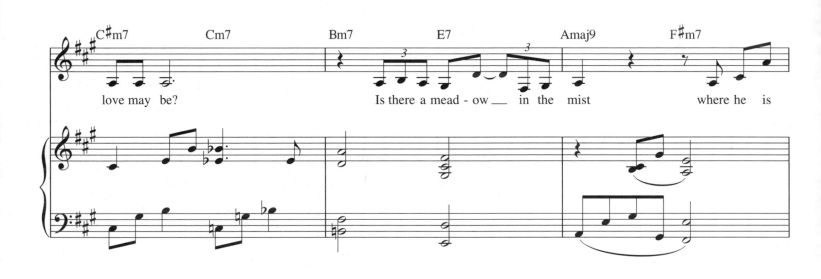

love may be? Is there a mead - ow __ in the mist where he is

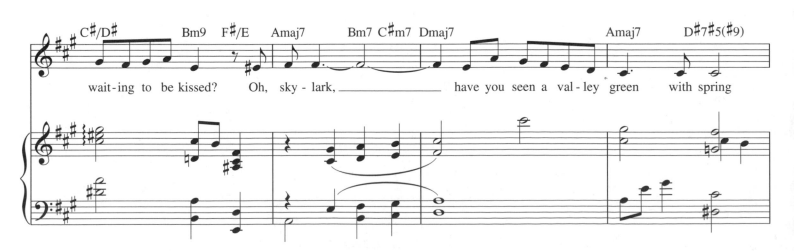

wait-ing to be kissed? Oh, sky - lark, ____ have you seen a val - ley green with spring

SOME CHILDREN SEE HIM

Lyric by WIHLA HUTSON
Music by ALFRED BURT

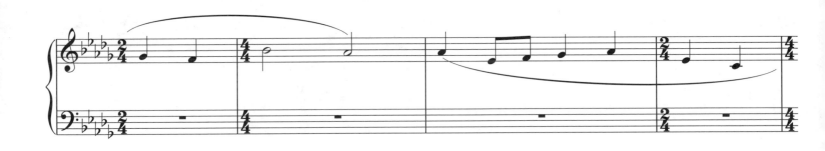

Some chil-dren see Him lil-y__ white the

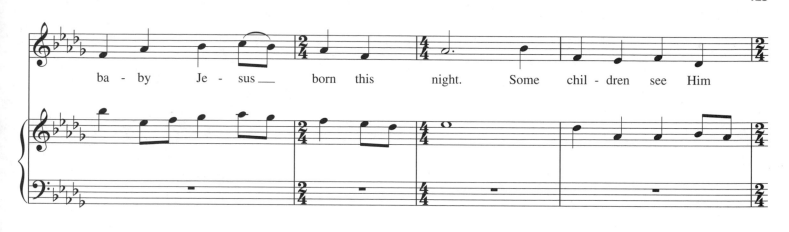

ba - by Je - sus __ born this night. Some chil - dren see Him

lil - y __ white with tress - es soft and __ fair. Some

chil - dren see Him __ bronzed and brown the Lord of heav - en to

earth come down. Some chil - dren see Him bronzed and __

brown with dark and heav-y___ hair. Some chil-dren see Him

al-mond-eyed this Sav-iour whom we___ kneel be-

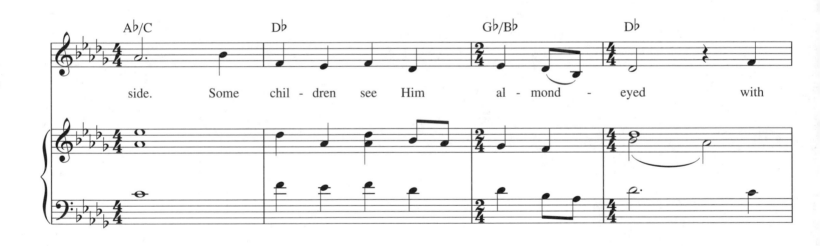

side. Some chil-dren see Him al-mond-eyed with

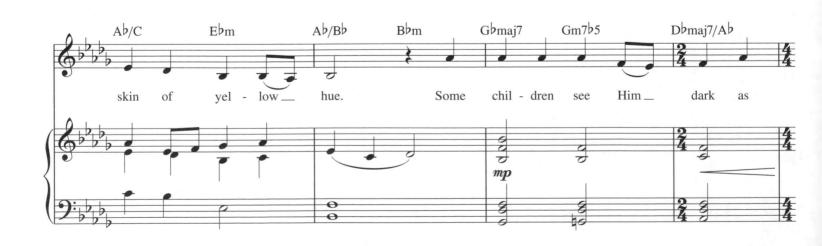

skin of yel-low___ hue. Some chil-dren see Him___ dark as

THE SURREY WITH THE FRINGE ON TOP

from OKLAHOMA!

Lyrics by OSCAR HAMMERSTEIN II
Music by RICHARD RODGERS

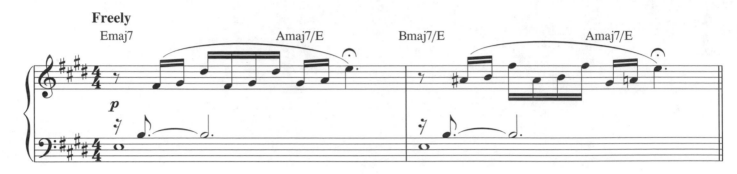

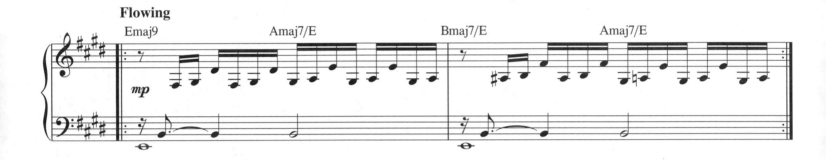

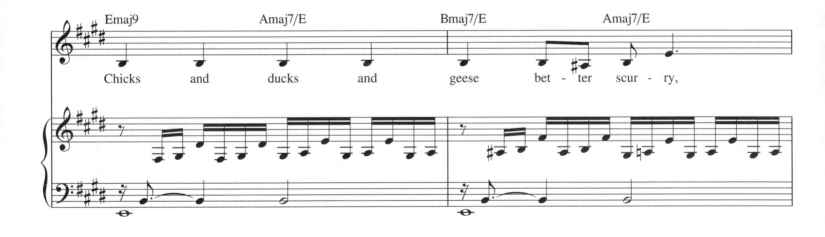

Chicks and ducks and geese bet-ter scur-ry,

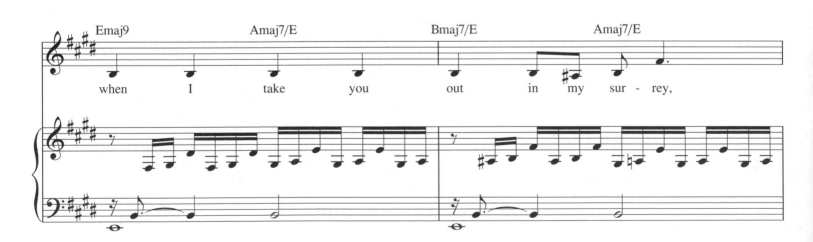

when I take you out in my sur-rey,

WE CAN BE KIND

Words and Music by
DAVID FRIEDMAN

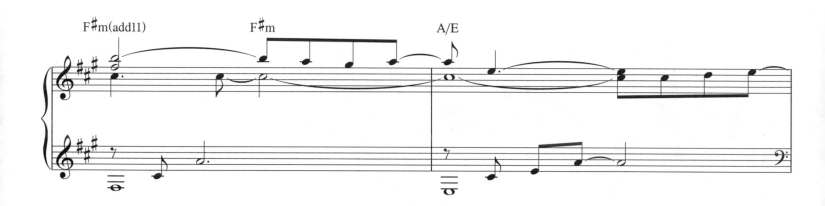

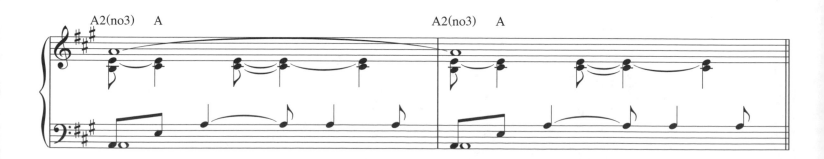

WE LIVE ON BORROWED TIME

Words and Music by
DAVID FRIEDMAN

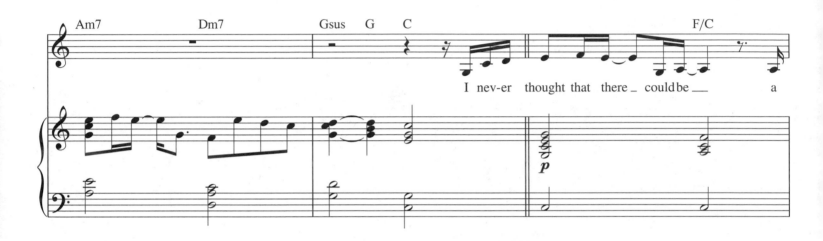

I nev-er thought that there could be a

love like yours and mine. I nev-er dreamed that I would see the

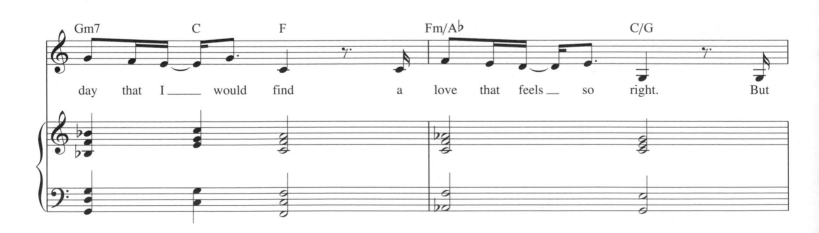

day that I would find a love that feels so right. But

ORIGINAL KEYS FOR SINGERS

MARIAH CAREY

Vocal transcriptions of all five octaves of this pop diva's 20 most popular tunes, including: Always Be My Baby • Dreamlover • Emotions • Heartbreaker • Hero • I Don't Wanna Cry • Love Takes Time • Loverboy • One Sweet Day • Vision of Love • We Belong Together • and more.
00306835 Vocal Transcriptions with Piano...$19.95

PATSY CLINE

The definitive Patsy Cline book for singers! 27 top songs in the original key, newly transcribed from the original recordings. For voice with piano accompaniment, with chord symbols. Includes: Always • Blue Moon of Kentucky • Crazy • Faded Love • I Fall to Pieces • Just a Closer Walk with Thee • Sweet Dreams • more. Also includes a biography.
00740072 Vocal Transcriptions with Piano...$14.95

ELLA FITZGERALD

Arguably the best female jazz singer ever, no one could out-swing or out-scat "The First Lady of Song." This fine book features authentic transcriptions in the original keys of 25 Fitzgerald classics in voice with piano accompaniment format: A-tisket, A-tasket • But Not for Me • Easy to Love • Embraceable You • The Lady Is a Tramp • Misty • Oh, Lady Be Good! • Satin Doll • Stompin' at the Savoy • Take the "A" Train • and more. Includes a biography and discography.
00740252 Vocal Transcriptions with Piano...$16.95

JOSH GROBAN

Alejate • Awake • Believe • February Song • In Her Eyes • L'Ultima Notte • Lullaby • Machine • Mai • Never Let Go • Now or Never • O Holy Night • Per Te • The Prayer • Remember When It Rained • So She Dances • To Where You Are • Un Amore Per Sempre • Un Dia Llegara • You Are Loved (Don't Give Up) • You Raise Me Up • You're Still You.
00306969 Vocal Transcriptions with Piano...$19.95

BILLIE HOLIDAY

TRANSCRIBED FROM HISTORIC RECORDINGS

This groundbreaking publication features authentic transcriptions in the original keys of 19 classics from the key signature recordings of the great Lady Day. Includes a biography and discography, and these standards in voice with piano accompaniment format: All of Me • Billie's Blues (I Love My Man) • Body and Soul • Crazy He Calls Me • Easy Living • Fine and Mellow • A Fine Romance • God Bless' the Child • Good Morning Heartache • I Cried for You • I Wished on the Moon • Lover, Come Back to Me • Miss Brown to You • Solitude • Some Other Spring • Strange Fruit • This Year's Kisses • The Very Thought of You • You've Changed. A must for every jazz singer's library!
00740140 Vocal Transcriptions with Piano...$16.95

DIANA KRALL

20 of the signature songs of jazz vocalist/pianist Diana Krall. Includes: All or Nothing at All • The Frim Fram Sauce • The Girl in the Other Room • Hit That Jive Jack • The Look of Love • 'S Wonderful • This Can't Be Love • and more.
00306743 Vocal Transcriptions with Piano...$19.95

THE BEST OF LIZA MINNELLI

And All That Jazz • But the World Goes 'Round • Cabaret • City Lights • Colored Lights • Losing My Mind • Maybe This Time • Me and My Baby • Mein Herr • Money Tree, The • My Own Best Friend • My Own Space • Theme from "New York, New York" • Nowadays • A Quiet Thing • Ring Them Bells • Sara Lee • Say Liza (Liza with a Z) • Shine It On • Sing Happy • The Singer • Sitting Pretty (The Money Song) • Stepping Out • Taking a Chance on Love.
00306928 Vocal Transcriptions with Piano...$19.95

THE VERY BEST OF FRANK SINATRA

40 swingin' Sinatra classic tunes arranged in their original keys. Includes: Come Fly with Me • I've Got You Under My Skin • It Was a Very Good Year • My Way • Night and Day • Summer Wind • The Way You Look Tonight • You Make Me Feel So Young • and more. Includes biography.
00306753 Vocal Transcriptions with Piano...$19.95

SARAH VAUGHAN

The *All Music Guide* calls Vaughan "one of the most wondrous voices of the 20th century." This collection gathers 25 of her classics arranged in her original keys so today's singers can try to match her performances. Songs include: Black Coffee • But Not for Me • Cherokee (Indian Love Song) • Darn That Dream • East of the Sun (And West of the Moon) • If You Could See Me Now • It Might as Well Be Spring • Lullaby of Birdland • The Man I Love • My Funny Valentine • The Nearness of You • A Night in Tunisia • Perdido • September Song • Tenderly • and more.
00306558 Vocal Transcriptions with Piano...$17.95

Prices, contents, and availability subject to change without notice.

Pro Vocal® Series
SONGBOOK & SOUND-ALIKE CD
SING 8 GREAT SONGS WITH A PROFESSIONAL BAND

Whether you're a karaoke singer or an auditioning professional, the Pro Vocal® series is for you! Unlike most karaoke packs, each book in the Pro Vocal Series contains the lyrics, melody, and chord symbols for eight hit songs. The CD contains demos for listening, and separate backing tracks so you can sing along. The CD is playable on any CD player, but it is also enhanced so PC and Mac computer users can adjust the recording to any pitch without changing the tempo! Perfect for home rehearsal, parties, auditions, corporate events, and gigs without a backup band.

WOMEN'S EDITIONS

00740409	**1. Broadway Standards**	$14.95
00740249	**2. Jazz Standards**	$14.95
00740246	**3. Contemporary Hits**	$14.95
00740277	**4. '80s Gold**	$12.95
00740299	**5. Christmas Standards**	$15.95
00740281	**6. Disco Fever**	$12.95
00740279	**7. R&B Super Hits**	$12.95
00740309	**8. Wedding Gems**	$12.95
00740409	**9. Broadway Standards**	$14.95
00740348	**10. Andrew Lloyd Webber**	$14.95
00740344	**11. Disney's Best**	$14.95
00740378	**12. Ella Fitzgerald**	$14.95
00740350	**14. Musicals of Boublil & Schönberg**	$14.95
00740377	**15. Kelly Clarkson**	$14.95
00740377	**16. Disney Favorites**	$14.95
00740353	**17. Jazz Ballads**	$12.95
00740376	**18. Jazz Vocal Standards**	$14.95
00740375	**20. Hannah Montana**	$16.95
00740354	**21. Jazz Favorites**	$12.95
00740374	**22. Patsy Cline**	$14.95
00740369	**23. Grease**	$14.95
00740367	**25. ABBA**	$14.95
00740365	**26. Movie Songs**	$14.95
00740360	**28. High School Musical 1 & 2**	$14.95
00740363	**29. Torch Songs**	$14.95
00740379	**30. Hairspray**	$14.95
00740380	**31. Top Hits**	$14.95
00740384	**32. Hits of the '70s**	$14.95
00740388	**33. Billie Holiday**	$14.95
00740389	**34. The Sound of Music**	$14.95
00740390	**35. Contemporary Christian**	$14.95
00740392	**36. Wicked**	$14.95
00740393	**37. More Hannah Montana**	$14.95
00740394	**38. Miley Cyrus**	$14.95
00740396	**39. Christmas Hits**	$15.95
00740410	**40. Broadway Classics**	$14.95
00740415	**41. Broadway Favorites**	$14.95
00740416	**42. Great Standards You Can Sing**	$14.95
00740417	**43. Singable Standards**	$14.95
00740418	**44. Favorite Standards**	$14.95
00740419	**45. Sing Broadway**	$14.95
00740420	**46. More Standards**	$14.95
00740421	**47. Timeless Hits**	$14.95
00740422	**48. Easygoing R&B**	$14.95

MEN'S EDITIONS

00740248	**1. Broadway Songs**	$14.95
00740250	**2. Jazz Standards**	$14.95
00740251	**3. Contemporary Hits**	$14.95
00740278	**4. '80s Gold**	$12.95
00740298	**5. Christmas Standards**	$15.95
00740280	**6. R&B Super Hits**	$12.95
00740282	**7. Disco Fever**	$12.95
00740310	**8. Wedding Gems**	$12.95
00740411	**9. Broadway Greats**	$14.95
00740333	**10. Elvis Presley – Volume 1**	$14.95
00740349	**11. Andrew Lloyd Webber**	$14.95
00740345	**12. Disney's Best**	$14.95
00740347	**13. Frank Sinatra Classics**	$14.95
00740334	**14. Lennon & McCartney**	$14.95
00740335	**15. Elvis Presley – Volume 2**	$14.95
00740343	**17. Disney Favorites**	$14.95
00740351	**18. Musicals of Boublil & Schönberg**	$14.95
00740346	**20. Frank Sinatra Standards**	$14.95
00740362	**27. Michael Bublé**	$14.95
00740361	**28. High School Musical 1 & 2**	$14.95
00740364	**29. Torch Songs**	$14.95
00740366	**30. Movie Songs**	$14.95
00740368	**31. Hip Hop Hits**	$14.95
00740370	**32. Grease**	$14.95
00740371	**33. Josh Groban**	$14.95
00740373	**34. Billy Joel**	$17.95
00740381	**35. Hits of the '50s**	$14.95
00740382	**36. Hits of the '60s**	$14.95
00740383	**37. Hits of the '70s**	$14.95
00740385	**38. Motown**	$14.95
00740386	**39. Hank Williams**	$14.95
00740387	**40. Neil Diamond**	$14.95
00740391	**41. Contemporary Christian**	$14.95
00740397	**42. Christmas Hits**	$15.95
00740399	**43. Ray**	$14.95
00740400	**44. The Rat Pack Hits**	$14.95
00740401	**45. Songs in the Style of Nat "King" Cole**	$14.95
00740402	**46. At the Lounge**	$14.95
00740403	**47. The Big Band Singer**	$14.95
00740404	**48. Jazz Cabaret Songs**	$14.95
00740405	**49. Cabaret Songs**	$14.95
00740406	**50. Big Band Standards**	$14.95
00740412	**51. Broadway's Best**	$14.95

MIXED EDITIONS

These editions feature songs for both male and female voices.

00740311	**1. Wedding Duets**	$12.95
00740398	**2. Enchanted**	$14.95
00740407	**3. Rent**	$14.95
00740408	**4. Broadway Favorites**	$14.95
00740413	**5. South Pacific**	$14.95
00740414	**6. High School Musical 3**	$14.95

FOR MORE INFORMATION, SEE YOUR LOCAL MUSIC DEALER, OR WRITE TO:

HAL•LEONARD® CORPORATION
7777 W. BLUEMOUND RD. P.O. BOX 13819 MILWAUKEE, WI 53213

Visit Hal Leonard online at www.halleonard.com

Prices, contents, & availability subject to change without notice.
Disney charaters and artwork © Disney Enterprises, Inc.

1008